"And what would you do ... if God spoke directly to your face and said, 'I command that you be happy in the world, as long as you live.' What would you do then?"

Richard Bach, ILLUSIONS

LISTEN TO WOMEN FOR A CHANGE:

EVERY WOMAN'S

HANDBOOK

CREATED BY

LEE BYRD & YVONNE KRANZ

UPPITY ♀ PUBLISHING

LISTEN TO WOMEN FOR A CHANGE:

EVERY WOMAN'S HANDBOOK

Published in the United States by Uppity ♀ Publishing
P.O. Box 789
Hotchkiss, Colorado 81419

A portion of the proceeds from the sale of this book will
be donated to the battered women's movement.

FIRST EDITION

ISBN 0-9644942-0-5

Design by Carol Jones

Prologue

If you've picked up this book, you're here for a reason. Do you often feel as though others run your life instead of you? Are you tired of it? Do you second-guess yourself and frequently experience difficulty in making decisions? Perhaps it's time to reclaim your power.

Every Woman's Handbook is a collection of inspirational poems, prose, and quotations designed to assist women on the road to self-determination. This handbook is unconventional. Although designed to read from front to back, it will work its magic however you read it. It's your book. Do with it what you please; we are not going to tell you how to use it. After all, other people's advice is what got you here in the first place, right?

What gives us the expertise to *suggest* this gathered group of quotations? We are former victims of violence perpetrated against us by men in our lives - men we trusted and loved. We had to make a conscious decision to turn our lives around, stop being victimized and reclaim our power. Sometimes it was hard to imagine getting through the day. That's when these verbal nuggets came in handy, especially when hung in obvious places where we saw them several times throughout the day. They were used as affirmations and when repeated over and over mentally and verbally, became our *new way of life*.

These maxims continued to be of benefit to us. For example, in the mid-eighties, we both worked for a women's resource center in northern California and used them as counseling tools when dealing with female victims of male violence.

Although our writings indicate that men are the perpetrators of violence against women and statistics confirm this fact, we by no means intend to disregard those who find themselves in violent lesbian relationships. Also, we do not wish to imply that gender is the greatest oppressor of women. Some women experience greater subordination as a result of race, class, sexual orientation, age, appearance, and/or physical/mental disabilities. Please translate gender as required.

Remember, your thinking is what got you here today. If you're happy, great. If not, you have the power to change it anytime you want. Often your thinking is a result of values imposed on you by others, rather than conscious thoughts decided on by you. You are free to change your life whenever you choose. So what are you waiting for? Begin your journey now. *Every Woman's Handbook* is small enough to keep with you when you need a good dose of support. Just open to any page and join the millions currently engaged in reclaiming their power.

Don't give up the fight women, for it's in the fight that we will find our strength. Stay strong and be safe.

Vonnie And Lee ♡✗o✗

Throughout The Handbook, you will find pages indicating "cut-along-the-dotted-lines." These are simply reminders and suggestions to clip your favorite words of wisdom, and hang them where they are frequently visible. We've also provided note pages to record your personal reflections. We hope the journal portion in the back of the book will inspire you to continue regular journal writing--always a good idea.

... there can be no really pervasive system of oppression,
such as that in the United States, without the consent of the oppressed.
Florynce R. Kennedy

WARNING!

Proceed with caution.
Freedom is not for the faint of heart.

Kay Leigh Hagan
Fugitive Information

What's a woman like you doing with a man like that?!

Overheard at an AAUW luncheon

The trouble with some women,
they get all excited about nothing.
And then they marry him.

Cher

WHAT'S LOVE GOT TO DO WITH IT?

TINA TURNER

Intimacy: You offer and are offered, validation, understanding, and a sense of being valued intellectually, emotionally and physically.

Janet G. Woititz
Struggle for Intimacy

When we value something, it has a positive tone. We prize it, cherish it, esteem it, <u>respect</u> it, hold it dear.

Louis E. Raths, Merrill Harmin, &
Sidney B. Simon, *Values and Teaching*

It takes a DAMN GOOD MAN TO BE BETTER THAN NONE.

♂

Misery demands company
have none of it!

∞ Leo Buscaglia

The only consolation I can find in your immediate presence is your ultimate absence.

Shelagh Delaney, Act 1, Scene 1
A Taste of Honey

"GET OFF ME BABY,
GET OFF AND LEAVE ME ALONE
I'M LONELY WHEN YOU'RE GONE
BUT I'M LONELIER
WHEN YOU'RE HOME ..."

"Get Off Me Baby" by Holly Near

Some of my loneliest nights were spent
in bed with my husband.

≥●

Just because you surround yourself with people/family
doesn't guarantee that you won't be

lonely
lonely
lonely
lonely
lonely
lonely
lonely
lonely
lonely

11

THERE'S NO SUCH THING AS A FREE LUNCH.

F-E-A-R

FALSE   EVIDENCE   APPEARING   REAL

NOTHING IS MORE DIFFICULT THAN COMPETING WITH A MYTH.

Francoise Giroud

My family needs me.

It's a woman's place to suffer!

My husband puts me on a pedestal!
(A pedestal is just as much a prison as any small space.)

A husband will take care of me.

Notes

Perspective - Use it or lose it.
Richard Bach, ILLUSIONS

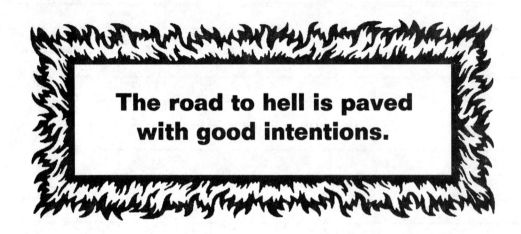

The road to hell is paved
with good intentions.

"As I grow older I pay less attention to what men say.
I just watch what they do."

Mae West

A lie tells you something profound about the liar.

It is the weak who are cruel, gentleness can only be expected from the strong.

Linda Ronstadt

People will treat you exactly the way you allow them to treat you.

No one can make you feel inferior
without your consent.

Eleanor Roosevelt

....shame kills faster than disease.

Buchi Emecheta

"You might as well fall flat on your face as lean over too far backward."

James Thurber

Friends are those who always encourage you to do your best

The bond that links your
true family is not one of blood,
but of respect and joy in each other's life.

Richard Bach, ILLUSIONS

People who say unkind things
aren't friends.

Who you are speaks so loudly
I can't hear what you are saying!

———◦◦◦———

Conflict arises when your
attachment to your beliefs
about what **Reality** *should* be
prevents you from accepting it as it is.

R. S. READ

The world's spiritual geniuses seem to discover universally that the mind's muddy river, this ceaseless flow of trivia and trash, cannot be dammed, and that trying to dam it is a waste of effort that might lead to madness.

Annie Dillard

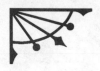

WHAT YOU THINK OF ME
IS NONE OF MY BUSINESS

Terry Cole-Whittaker

I have no creative use for guilt, yours or my own. Guilt is only another way of avoiding informed action, of buying time out of the pressing need to make clear choices, out of the approaching storm that can feed the earth as well as bend the trees.

Audre Lorde

THERE ARE ONLY TWO WAYS TO HANDLE GUILT:

1. Stop what it is that makes you feel guilty
2. Stop feeling guilty for what you are doing

You cannot intend to get something
which is unavailable.

To pretend you can is a lie.
To pretend you can is insane.

R. S. READ

If something doesn't work
to support your life,
have none of it!

                                         ∽ Leo Buscaglia

"The softminded person wants to freeze
the moment and hold life
in the gripping yoke of sameness."

Reverend Martin Luther King

...we do not have to become prisoners of our perspectives;
we can change them and our lives by developing a
completely new world picture ... one human step at a time.

Barry Neil Kaufman, *Happiness Is A Choice*

Take short steps.
Often times we fail simply because
we try to take too BIG a step too quickly.

Nothing heals like time ...

Baby steps!

Baby steps!

Baby steps!

To suffer without learning from it
is absolute stupidity.

℗ Leo Buscaglia

You can trust people to be exactly who they are.

R. S. READ

And then there's the guy
who promises everything...

...while he's patting your butt!
...don't ya just hate that?!

All the King's horses and all the King's
men couldn't put Humpty together again.

If you hang out with shit, you're gonna get some on ya!

You never really know someone

till you divorce them.

Living well is the best revenge.

TIME WOUNDS ALL HEELS!

Jane Ace "Easy Aces" Radio Show

"Yesterday we stumbled across the first recorded history of when humankind made an ass of itself. Then we discovered when humankind first laughed. Guess what! We first laughed the day we first made an ass of ourselves."

-Trudy the Bag Lady

Lilly Tomlin, *The Search for Signs of Intelligent Life in the Universe.*

Difficulties are meant to rouse,
not discourage.

A cloudburst doesn't last all day.

George Harrison

There is no problem so big
that it cannot be run away from.

Richard Bach, ILLUSIONS

And this too shall pass.

"Sometimes to keep it together
you've got to leave it alone..."

The Eagles, Wasted Time

**Constant togetherness is fine
but only for Siamese twins**

Victoria Billings

To love something means to allow
it to be the way it is and the way it is not.

R. S. Read

Loving and accepting something doesn't mean
you have to live in an abusive situation.

You are not responsible
for the good will of everyone you meet.

Laura C. Martin
A LIFE WITHOUT FEAR

Trying to control
the uncontrollable
is exhausting
and frustrating!

Anne Wilson Schaef

Remember your illusion of control
is just that — an illusion.

Anne Wilson Schaef

That the Birds of
Worry and Care
Fly about your
Head, This you
Cannot Change,
But that they build
Nests in your hair,
This you can prevent
— Chinese Proverb

Nothing fixes a thing so intensely in the memory
as the wish to forget it.

Michel de Montaigne, 1533-1592

Some of your hurts you have cured, And the sharpest you even survived, But what torments of grief you've endured, From evils which never arrived.

Emerson

Real strength deals with reality.

Some life situations are not ours to understand
but rather to accept and move forward...
...Understanding is the booby prize!

To know and not to do
is not really yet to know.

Buddhist teaching

S hips are safe inside the harbor
    but is that what ships are for?

"I tore myself away from the safe comfort of certain ties through my love for truth; and truth rewarded me."

Simone de Beauvoir

Fix your thoughts on what is true
and good and right.

Philippians 4:8

When nothing is sure,
everything is possible.

Margaret Drabble

When you start to see that your life is
filled with choices you begin to acknowledge
your own personal reality.

R.S. Read

ASK YOURSELF...

✓ What's wrong with this picture?

✓ Is what I'm doing for my life working?

✓ If not, why not and what can I change?

✓ Am I willing to do what it takes to get what I want?

✓ Am I listening to myself?

✓ Am I taking care of myself?

Notes

Clarify what you want

No one around you
will carry the blame for you.
Only you'll arrive at your own made end,
with no one but yourself to be offended;
it's you who decides.

-V

**Everything you do
is a reflection of your integrity.**

You cannot jump backward and forward simultaneously.

R. S. Read

Trust Life
Move Ahead

Go as far as you can see, and when you get there, you will always be able to see farther.

You are not the depression you have.
You are not the marriage you resist.

R.S. Read

Those hurts and pains that we experience in childhood don't just magically evaporate as we grow older. They rumble around in us, and when we have reached a level of strength, maturity, insight, and awareness to handle them, they come up to be worked through. This is one of the ways our inner being is loving to us. It gives us every opportunity to heal the hurts we need to heal, and it gives us that opportunity when we are strong enough to handle it.

Anne Wilson Schaef

"It isn't for the moment you are struck that you need courage, but for the long uphill climb back to sanity and faith and security."

Anne Morrow Lindberg,
Hour of Gold, Hour of Lead

A new philosophy, a way of life, is not given for nothing.   It has to be paid dearly for and only acquired with much patience and great effort.

Fyodor Dostoyevsky

Keep Breathing!

Sophie Tucker

If it's to be it's up to me.

"In search of my lost innocence I walked out a door.
At the time I believed I was looking for a purpose, but
I found instead the meaning of choice."

Liv Ullmann

Choice! The key is *choice*. You have options.
You need not spend your life wallowing in failure,
ignorance, grief, poverty, shame, and self-pity.

But, hold on!
If this is true then why have so many among us
apparently elected to live in that manner?
The answer is obvious. Those who live in
unhappy failure have never exercised their
options for a better way of life because
they have never been aware that they had any choices!

Og Mandino, *The Choice*

...if you don't grow up feeling that you ever have any choices, you don't have the sense that you have emotional responsibility.

Carol Gilligan, *In a Different Voice*

At this instant your life is as good
as you've been willing to have it be.
How much better are you willing to have it...?

R. S. Read

"Life's not fair! Life's not fair!" she cried.
"A fair's a place you go to ride rides,"
the Goddess replied.

If you insist in believing Life is
conflict, pain, and hate,
It will be conflict, pain, and hate.

R. S. Read

Our expectancies not only affect how we
see reality, but also affect the reality itself.

Edward E. Jones

The only way an individual can rise above the picture she has of herself is to change that picture, because the way you see yourself is exactly the way you will be. Whatever picture you paint in your mind, the mind goes to work to complete.

What you do reflects your values.

You cannot perform in a manner
inconsistent with the way
you see yourself.

If you think you can, or you
think you can't,
you're right.

If you don't see yourself
as a winner,
you cannot perform
as a winner.

By choosing to feel good about yourself and your life,
to have a higher self-image, and to see that your
own needs are met, you are more able
to relate to others in
a healthy way.

Positive thinking will let you do everything better
than negative thinking will.

If you're looking at the sun,
you will seldom see any shadows.
Helen Keller

Choose to Love
Choose to Live

Your thoughts are the blueprint of your future.

Optimum Health Institute of San Diego

YOU MAY NOT BE RESPONSIBLE
FOR BEING DOWN,
BUT YOU MUST
BE RESPONSIBLE FOR GETTING UP.

It's not what you've got,
it's how you use it!

You create your own reality.

...living life fully is not a task,
but rather a grand opportunity.

Anne Wilson Schaef

"Peace comes from
your commitment to learn about you."

R. S. Read

When we realize we don't know,
we are open to what we don't know.

Anne Wilson Schaef

In order to get ahead,
you have to use one.

Anne Wilson Schaef

KNOWLEDGE IS POWER.

☞ Sit down and read.
Educate yourself for the coming
conflicts.

Mother Jones as quoted in Ms., Nov. '81

☞ Only fools refuse to be taught.

Proverbs 1:7

☞ Children pay more attention to
what you do than what you say.

Mama Ziglar

"Courage is the price that Life
exacts for granting peace."

Amelia Earhart

It really is up to you.

Marjorie Hansen Shaevitz
The Superwoman Syndrome

Life's too short!
Life's too short!
Life's too short!

Raquel Silreyra (student in philosophia class)

Here today, gone tomorrow,
so don't get attached to things.

❀ Maude

Conflict arises out of attachments to the Past.

R. S. Read

Beliefs and convictions reach out
from the past, and they
cannot be altered by fervent desire alone.

Raisa Davydovna Orlova

Our greatest resistance is the resistance to change.

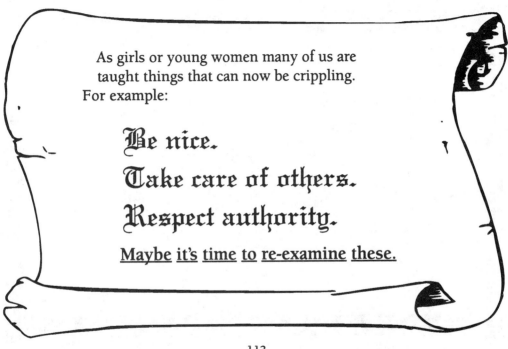

As girls or young women many of us are taught things that can now be crippling. For example:

Be nice.

Take care of others.

Respect authority.

<u>Maybe</u> <u>it's</u> <u>time</u> <u>to</u> <u>re-examine</u> <u>these.</u>

113

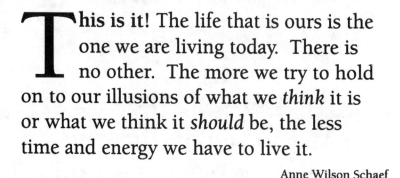

This is it! The life that is ours is the one we are living today. There is no other. The more we try to hold on to our illusions of what we *think* it is or what we think it *should* be, the less time and energy we have to live it.

Anne Wilson Schaef

Just because others have always
decided what's best for you
doesn't mean you are incapable
of deciding for yourself.

If we cannot love ourselves, how can we love anyone else?

LOVE IS ...

♥ *Self-communication*

♥ *Conscious mutual support*

♥ *Never jealous nor boastful*

♥ *Never arrogant or rude*

♥ *Never coercive*

Notes

... do not exist to impress the world.
Richard Bach, ILLUSIONS

As long as we are dependent on others
for our self-image or our self-esteem,
we will remain without any
sense of our own self-worth.
We remain totally powerless
and not in control of our own lives.

The thing you have to be prepared for
is that other people don't always dream your dream.

Linda Ronstadt

Who I am is what fulfills me...

Audre Lorde

"One's philosophy is not best expressed in words,
it is expressed in the choices one makes...
In the long run, we shape our lives and we shape
ourselves. The process never ends until we die.
And the Choices we make are ultimately <u>our</u> responsibility."

Eleanor Roosevelt

Change the beliefs and we change the attitudes,
thoughts, feelings and behaviors that come from them.

Barry Neil Kaufman

My silences
had not
protected me.

Audre Lorde

Ignorance is not bliss
— it's oblivion.

Phillip Wylie

Assertive people communicate directly and honestly, are more concerned with achieving results than avoiding mistakes, and know that confrontation is inevitable and can be a useful part of growth.

Laura Martin

Live never to be ashamed if anything you do
or say is published around the world
— even if what is published is not true.

Richard Bach, ILLUSIONS

Hold Your Head High
&
Remember Who You Damn Are!

Bonnie Whitener

You've got it all!!

But only when you start to acknowledge
it, is it going to get interesting. Your problem
is you're afraid to acknowledge your own beauty.
You're too busy holding on to your unworthiness.

One is not born a genius, one becomes a genius.

Simone de Beauvoir

Don't let life happen to you, you must happen to life.

"In order to live free and happy,
you must sacrifice boredom,
it's not always an easy sacrifice."

Richard Bach, ILLUSIONS

It is in the knowledge of the genuine conditions of our
lives that we must draw our strength to live
and our reasons for acting.

Simone de Beauvoir

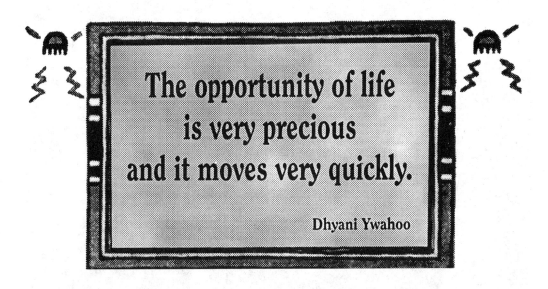

The opportunity of life
is very precious
and it moves very quickly.

Dhyani Ywahoo

... reach for our lives
...for *all* life
...deep into the
cosmos that is our own souls.

Sonia Johnson

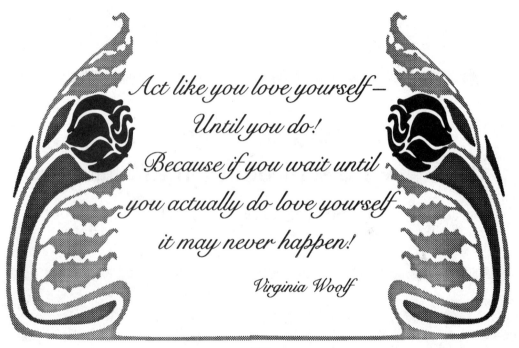

Act like you love yourself—
Until you do!
Because if you wait until
you actually do love yourself
it may never happen!

Virginia Woolf

"If I am not for myself,
who will be for me?"
If not now, when?

The Talmud

You must do the thing you think you cannot do.

Eleanor Roosevelt

"A good laugh is good for the spirits it's true,
But a good cry is good for the soul."

Bette Midler, *The Saga of Baby Divine*

SELF-CARE

To keep a lamp burning we have to keep putting oil in it.

Mother Teresa

CONCEIVE .... BELIEVE .... ACHIEVE

Ways to take care of yourself:

▼ Nurture yourself

▼ NEVER do what you hate

▼ Believe in Hope - Live your dream

▼ Remember, NO means NO!

▼ Feel free to say: That's not my job.

▼ Give it everything you got!

▼ Don't cling! Just don't!!

▼ Never settle

139

SELF-CARE

▼ Just show up
▼ Don't agonize — Organize
           Florynce R. Kennedy

▼ Always be honest with yourself

▼ Acknowledge and Reward your own efforts

▼ Raise more hell and fewer dahlias!
           Emma Goldman

▼ Solitude is not a luxury. It's a right and a necessity.
           Anne Wilson Schaef

▼ Fresh flowers in your office/home add a luxurious touch.

▼ Invest in yourself

▼ Do what works

▼ Try something new each day

Notes

REMEMBER WHAT THE DORMOUSE SAID,
"FEED YOUR HEAD, FEED YOUR HEAD, FEED YOUR HEAD." Grace Slick

TAKE A VACATION!

We owe it to ourselves and those around us to take vacations. This doesn't have to mean you leave home on some expensive jaunt (although that's not a bad idea!). It could be as simple as slipping away for a few minutes by yourself. For example, some suggested "mini" vacations might be:

- ✓ A "night off" without the kids
- ✓ An uninterrupted bubble bath
- ✓ An early morning or late evening walk alone or with a close friend
- ✓ Picnic in a special place such as by the beach or near a stream alone or with a close friend
- ✓ Take yourself out to a special place for lunch
- ✓ Take time to read something special

Taking time for ourselves can be a rewarding and empowering experience. It can help us clarify just what we want so that we can make healthier decisions.

Anne Wilson Schaef

Notes

FUN CAN CHANGE PEOPLE!

IT IS ALWAYS YOUR RESPONSIBILITY TO:

1. Be clear about what you want.
2. Maintain your integrity.
3. Make valuable use of your time.
4. Be the strongest person you can be.
5. Seek out wise counsel.
6. Be true to yourself first.
7. Establish clear boundaries and honor them.
8. Learn how to say no.
9. Develop self-love.
10. Learning to recognize when it's their responsibility.
11. Love yourself.
12. Be safe.
13. Be proud of who you are.
14. Live life to the fullest every minute of everyday.

IT IS NEVER YOUR RESPONSIBILITY TO:

1. Give what you really don't want to give.
2. Sacrifice your integrity to anyone.
3. Do more than you have time to do.
4. Drain your strength for others.
5. Listen to unwise counsel.
6. Retain an unfair relationship.
7. Conform to unreasonable demands.
8. Put up with unpleasant situations.
9. Please unpleasant people.
10. Bear the burden of another's misbehavior.
11. Love unlovable people.
12. Feel guilty.
13. Submit to overbearing conditions.
14. Apologize for being yourself.
15. Meekly let life pass you by.

However confused the scene of our life appears,
however torn we may be who now do face that scene,
it can be faced, and we can go on to be whole.

Muriel Rukeyser

**THE DARKEST NIGHT SINCE THE
BEGINNING OF TIME
DID NOT TURN OUT ALL THE STARS.**

There are no endings ...
only new beginnings.

The Grateful Dead

What the caterpillar calls the end of the world,
the master calls a butterfly.

Richard Bach, ILLUSIONS

The Goddess is everywhere
because She likes you.

Father Sarducci

The light at
the end of the tunnel
is **NOT** a train.

Faith is a knowledge in the heart
beyond the reach of proof.

Argue for your limitations
and sure enough, they're yours.

Richard Bach, ILLUSIONS

Once you've been No. 1,
you can never be satisfied with less.

Chris Evert Lloyd

Only she who attempts the aↁↁↁↁↁↁ can achieve the impossible.

Robin Morgan
Ms Magazine

You are never given a wish without also
being given the power to make it true.
You may have to work for it, however.

Richard Bach, ILLUSIONS

Don't be an "IF" thinker,
be a "HOW" thinker.

Mary Crowley

The biggest sin is sitting on your ass.

Florynce Kennedy

Perhaps for some of you... I am the face of one of your fears. Because I am woman, because I am Black, because I am lesbian, because I am myself - a Black woman warrior poet doing my work - come to ask you, are you doing yours?

Audre Lorde

It isn't the situation that makes you happy,
it's you who makes you happy.

∽ Leo Buscaglia

"If you want to be high, be high,
if you want to be low, be low.
There's a million things to be
you know that there are."

❀ Maude

"MAKE SURE THAT YOUR LIFE IS A RARE ENTERTAINMENT!
IT DOESN'T TAKE ANYTHING DRASTIC.
YOU NEEDN'T BE GORGEOUS OR WEALTHY OR SMART
JUST VERY ENTHUSIASTIC!"

Bette Midler

MAKE THINGS HAPPEN INSTEAD OF LETTING THEM HAPPEN.

IT TAKES GUTS TO
LEAVE THE RUTS!

"If you want to change your life,
do it flamboyantly
and start immediately."

William James

JUST DO IT!

NIKE

166

We do not stop working and playing
because we grow old.
We grow old because we stop working and playing.

"Don't be afraid your life will end:
be afraid it will never begin."

Grace Hansen

L - I - V - E.

Live.

Otherwise you got nothing to talk about in the locker room.

❀ Maude

CELEBRATE LIFE!

No number of good deeds can make up
for a life not lived.

Anne Wilson Schaef

"Life is short, play hard."

Reebok

Winning isn't everything,
but losing sucks!

The first act of liberation
is to demand back our own heads.

Raya Dunayevskaya, "We Speak in Many Voices,"
Notes on Women's Liberation, 1970.

"Well I know it wasn't you who held me down;
heaven knows it wasn't you who set me free!
So often times it happens that we live our lives
in chains and we never even know
we have the key."

The Eagles

It can be very powerful to let go of self-pity,
judgements, feelings of unworthiness,
and feelings of inadequacy.

WE ARE WHAT WE REPEATEDLY DO. EXCELLENCE, THEN, IS NOT AN ACT, BUT A HABIT.

This is YOUR life ...
Are you paying attention?

It's awesome when we start
demanding what we are worth.

You need not apologize for being brilliant, talented, gorgeous, rich, or smart. Your success doesn't take away from anyone else's. It actually increases the possibility that others can have it too. Your money increases your capacity to give money to others, your joy increases your capacity to give joy to others, and your love increases your capacity to give love to others. Your playing small serves no one. It is a sick game. It is old thinking, and it is dire for the planet.

Stop it immediately.

Marianne Williamson
A Woman's Worth

Doubt indulged
soon becomes doubt realized.

Frances Ridley Havergal

Know what you want and commit to having it.

R. S. Read

*One person with a commitment
is worth more than a hundred
who only have an interest.*

Mary Crowley

You've got to pay attention!

Shoot for the moon
and even if you only make the tree tops
at least you're off the ground.

The World steps aside to let any woman past
if she knows where she's going.

Act as if it were impossible to fail.

I can do whatever must be done.

Chant from the great Goddess

Behind every successful Woman
is Herself

188

To love what you do and feel that it matters —
how could anything be more fun?

Katharine Graham

Exercise caution while making up your own mind,
as always.

Jane Smiley, *A Thousand Acres* (Rose said this)

"You will become
as small as your controlling desire;
as great as your dominant aspiration."

James Allen

The Great thing in the world is not so much
where we are but in what direction we are going.

Oliver Wendell Holmes

*I*f we women are ever to pull ourselves out of the morass of self-pity, self-destruction and impotence which has been our heritage for so long as we can remember, then it is perhaps even more important that we be supportive of each other's achievements and successes and strengths, than it is for us to be compassionate and understanding of each other's failures and weaknesses.

Anselma dell'Olio

Never forget that when we are silent, we are one.
And when we speak, we are two.

Indira Gandhi

We are powerful because we have survived,
and that is what it's all about
— survival and growth.

Audre Lorde

You can't kill the spirit
It's like a mountain
old and strong; it lives on and on.

—Naomi Littlebear, "Like a Mountain"

One of the effects of selling ourselves short is that
it slowly erodes our integrity.
We see ourselves doing things that compromise
our value system and we say nothing.
We act in ways not in keeping with our own personal morality.

Anne Wilson Schaef

It isn't easy to be a woman in a time like ours ...
but one thing never changes - the obligation to be
true to one's self whatever that truth may be.

I cannot and will not cut my conscience
to fit this year's fashions.

Lillian Hellman

A virtuous woman
is someone who is herself.

Anne Wilson Schaef

Take care of yourself,
if you don't who will?
Save yourself,
if you don't who will?

SELF-DEFENSE

Women deserve to live in safety and dignity. Male violence against women in any form is unacceptable. Our righteous outrage on behalf of our own precious selves must lead us first to take measures to insure our personal survival. To build a utopia, it helps to be alive.

Fugitive Information

Woman must not depend on the protection of man but must be taught to defend herself.

Susan B. Anthony 1871

To defend yourself successfully, you have to believe you are worth defending.

Laura C. Martin

Notes

Respect Yourself

MORE SELF-DEFENSE

from

A Life Without Fear

Laura Martin

- Sign up for a self-defense class today!

- When it comes down to saving your own life you can't be too direct, too demanding, too selfish. Manners have nothing to do with survival.

- You *can* make a difference. You must use your knowledge and skills to keep safe.

- When you are feeling the lowest is when you need to be most alert to danger.

- If you experience a strong feeling when you first meet someone, pay attention to it.

- Your inner angel is a feeling within you that warns of danger. Learn to listen to it. Your life may depend on it.

Add her book to your library today!

What I have, I only have for now, this instant.
In the next instant it may be gone - that's life's game.
Is it time to realize my life with my mate is over?
Pick up from here, with my own life.
If I stay with him I know what it'll be like,
the worrying and the hassles,
the plans that never seem to happen.

Vonnie in contemplating leaving Tom

It [may seem] easier to live through someone else than to become complete yourself.
The freedom to lead and plan your own life is frightening if you have never faced it before.

Betty Friedan
The Feminine Mystique

The life you live should be your own!

By myself and LOVING it!

Be nobody's darling;
Be an outcast.

Alice Walker

When we put forth our perceptions, we are told that we don't understand reality. When we put forth our values, we are told that we are crazy and we just don't understand the way the world works. Is it any wonder that we sometimes have trouble with self-esteem?

Anne Wilson Schaef

One must talk. That's how it is. One must.

Marguerite Duras

**Women are stronger,
faster,
smarter,
and more powerful
than we give ourselves credit for being.**

Laura Martin

By failing to recognize your **potential**
you could be depriving yourself of **success.**

Confrontation doesn't always bring a
solution to the problem,
but until you confront the problem,
there will be no solution.

James Baldwin

Nothing is forever.

ONE DOESN'T GET LIBERATED BY HIDING.

Rita Mae Brown

It's not that [The Goddess] wants us to suffer. But suffering directs our attention to things we don't want to face and think about when we will not learn through gentler means.

John White

"I have more confidence than I do talent, and I think that confidence is the main achiever of success."

Dolly Parton

Outstanding people have
one thing in common:
an absolute sense of mission.

When your inner strength is realized and activated you become an inventive, daring, self-expressive being. You are interesting and valued by others.

Like water which can clearly mirror the sky and the trees only so long as its surface is undisturbed, the mind can only reflect the true image of the Self when it is tranquil and wholly relaxed.

Indra Devi

i found god in myself
& i loved her/i loved her fiercely

Ntozake Shange, "a laying on of hands"

YOU ARE THE ONLY PERSON ON THIS EARTH WHO CAN USE YOUR ABILITY.

...much of the world's sorrow comes from people who are this, yet allow themselves to be treated as that.

❀ Maude

I'm not Cinderella. I can't force
my foot into the glass slipper.

Lee Miller

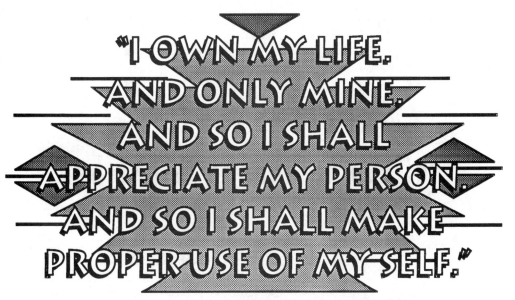

"I OWN MY LIFE.
AND ONLY MINE.
AND SO I SHALL
APPRECIATE MY PERSON.
AND SO I SHALL MAKE
PROPER USE OF MY SELF."

Ruth Beebe Hill
"'Hanta Yo': The Book of the Indian"

Failure is not fatal,
failure to change might be.

Coach John Wooden
U.C.L.A.

Make failure your teacher,
not your undertaker.

We don't pay the price for success,
we pay the price for failure.

Success

is dependent upon the glands
- sweat glands.

When you win, nothing hurts.

Joe Namath

I don't sing because I am happy,
I am happy because I sing!

There've been 11 billion people to walk this earth, but there's never been one like you.

YOU ARE UNIQUE!

Now, repeat ... I _____ am unique!
                    (Insert Your Name)
Rx: Repeat several times an hour every day of your life!

LOVE YOURSELF!
If you don't, who will?

BELIEVE IN YOURSELF!
If you don't, who will?

Most folks are about as happy
as they make up their minds to be.

Abraham Lincoln

CONSTANT COMPLAINTS NEVER WIN THE LOTTERY.

☞ Rule #1—Don't sweat the small stuff

☞ Rule #2—It's all small stuff

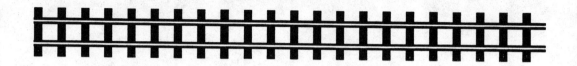

"Bear with me. I'll get back on the track.
Actually I'm not off the track.
I'm off the train, but not off the track."

Ruth Beebe Hill

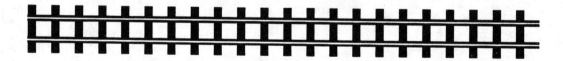

So...

What are you gonna do
with what you got?

Present Yourself

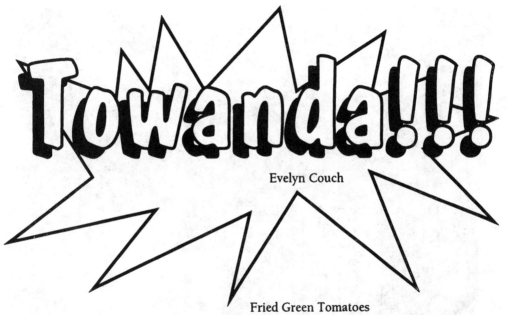

Towanda!!!

Evelyn Couch

Fried Green Tomatoes
At The Whistle Stop Cafe by Fannie Flagg

243

Uppity Women Unite

Epilogue

Too much of a good thing
can be wonderful!

Mae West

Please, Goddess,
teach us to laugh again;
but, don't ever let us
forget that we cried.

The clouds gathered together, stood still and watched the river scuttle around the forest floor, crash head long into the haunches of hills with no notion of where it was going, until exhausted, ill and grieving, it slowed to a stop just twenty leagues short of the sea.

Toni Morrison

Hangeth In There

Journal Pages

♡xox

Journal Pages

♡xox

Journal Pages

♡xox

Journal Pages

♥xox

Journal Pages

♡xox

Journal Pages

If you'd like to share how
Every Woman's Handbook
has affected your life,
we'd love to hear from you.

Uppity ♀ Publishing
P.O. Box 789
Hotchkiss, Colorado 81419

WITH GRATITUDE
(* Denotes Suggested Reading Material)

Carol Jones for her patience, her enthusiasm, and her creativity.

Karl Halfman for his wit, wisdom and the terrific research job he did!

Joyce Woods, she's the only person we know who can fill in all the squares of a crossword puzzle.

Mary Oishi for her expertise and encouragement.

Kevin Kranz and Craig Dawson for their support...financial and otherwise...

Women's International League for Peace and Freedom, 1213 Race St., Philadelphia, PA. For allowing us use of their logo: "Listen to Women for a Change."

Alice Walker. Excerpt from "Be Nobody's Darling," REVOLUTIONARY PETUNIAS & OTHER POEMS, Copyright © 1972, Alice Walker, reprinted by permission of Harcourt Brace & Co.

Anne Morrow Lindbergh, from Hour of Gold, Hour of Lead: Diaries and Letters of Anne Morrow Lindbergh 1929-1932. Copyright © 1973 by Anne Morrow Lindbergh. Harcourt Brace & Co.

Anne Roe. The Making of a Scientist. Greenwood Publishing Group, Westport, CT.

*Anne Wilson Schaef. Meditations for Women Who Do Too Much Calendar. Copyright © 1993. Workman Publishing Company, NY.

Annie Dillard. Pilgrim At Tinker Creek. Copyright © 1974. Harper's Magazine Foundation, NY.

Antony Miller. The Lives of Lee Miller. Copyright © 1985. Thames and Hudson, NY. Reprinted by permission of the publisher.

*Audre Lorde. Sister Outsider. Copyright © 1984, Audre Lorde. The Crossing Press Feminist Series, Freedom, CA.

*Barry Neil Kaufman. Happiness Is A Choice. Copyright © 1991. Ballantine/Fawcett Books, NY.

Bette Midler. <u>The Saga of Baby Divine.</u> Copyright © 1983. Crown Publishers Inc., NY.

Betty Friedan. <u>The Feminine Mystique.</u> Copyright © 1963 by Betty Friedan. Dell Publishing Co., Inc., NY.

Buchi Emecheta. <u>The Rape of Shavi.</u> Copyright © 1985. Geo. Braziller, Inc., NY.

Carol Gilligan. <u>In a Different Voice.</u> Copyright © 1982. Harvard University Press, Cambridge, MA. Reprinted by permission of the publishers.

*Eleanor Roosevelt. <u>You Learn By Living.</u> Copyright © 1960 by Eleanor Roosevelt, copyright renewed 1988 by Franklin A. Roosevelt. And <u>This Is My Story.</u> Copyright © 1939. Reprinted by permission of HarperCollins Publishers, Inc., NY.

Evelyn Couch as quoted in <u>Fried Green Tomatoes at the Whistle Stop Cafe</u> by Fannie Flagg. Copyright © 1987, Fannie Flagg. Random House, Inc., NY.

*Florynce R. Kennedy. "The Verbal Karate of Florynce R. Kennedy, Esq." by Gloria Steinem Ms. Magazine, March 1973, Copyright © 1973

Frances Ridley Havergal. From "The Imagination of the Thoughts of the Heart," <u>Royal Bounty.</u>

Francoise Giroud. <u>I Give You My Word.</u> Copyright © 1974. Houghton Mifflin, Boston.

Grace Slick. "White Rabbit," <u>Surrealistic Pillow</u> by the Jefferson Airplane. Copyright © 1967. RCA The Grateful Dead, Warner Bros. Records, Burbank, CA.

*Holly Near. "Get Off Me Baby." Redwood Records, Ukiah, CA.

Hortense Calisher. <u>Herself.</u> Copyright © 1972. Arbor House/Morrow Publishing, NY

Indira Gandhi. As quoted in "Conversation with Indira Gandhi," by Jose-Luis de Vilallonga, Oui Magazine. Copyright © 1974.

Indra Devi. From Ch. 1 of <u>Renewing Your Life Through Yoga.</u> Copyright © 1963.

James Thurber. "The Bear Who Let It Alone," <u>Fables for Our Time.</u> Copyright © 1940 James Thurber. Copyright © 1968 Helen Thurber. HarperCollins Publishers, Inc., NY.

Jane Ace. <u>The Fine Art of Hypochondria</u> by Goodman Ace. Copyright © 1966. Doubleday, NY.

Jane Smiley. <u>A Thousand Acres.</u> Copyright © 1992. Random House, Inc., NY.

*Katharine Graham. *"The Power That Didn't Corrupt"* by Jane Howard, Ms., Oct. 1974, Copyright © 1994.

*Kay Leigh Hagan. <u>Fugitive Information Essays From A Feminist Hothead.</u> Copyright © 1993 by Kay Leigh Hagan. HarperCollins Publishers, NY.

*Laura Martin. <u>A Life Without Fear: A Guide to Preventing Sexual Assault</u>. Copyright © 1992 by Laura Martin. Reproduced by permission of Rutledge Hill Press, Nashville, TN.

*Leo Buscaglia. These words of wisdom came from a variety of works by Leo. We acknowledge and appreciate his work and recommend it highly. (Thanks Leo!)

Lillian Hellman. From "Letters to the House Committee on Un-American Activities," <u>The Nation</u>, 31 May 1952.

*Lilly Tomlin from <u>The Search for Signs of Intelligent Life in the Universe</u> by Jane Wagner. Copyright © 1986, Jane Wagner. Harper & Row, NY.

Linda Ronstadt. Warner Bros. Records. Also as quoted in <u>Ronstadt Backed Into Her Notoriety</u> by Lawrence DeVine, Knight-Ridder Newspaper, 3 Oct. 1986.

Liv Ullmann. <u>Choices.</u> Copyright © 1984 by Liv Ullmann. Knopf, dist. by Random House, Inc., NY.

Louis E. Raths, Merrill Harmin, & Sidney B. Simon. <u>Values & Teaching: Working With Values In The Classroom.</u> Copyright © 1966. Values, Sunderland, MA. Published with the permission of the authors.

*Marianne Williamson. <u>A Woman's Worth.</u> Copyright © 1993. Random House, Inc., NY.

Margaret Drabble. The Middle Ground. Copyright © 1980. Random House, Inc., NY.

Marguerite Duras. The Vice-Consul. Copyright © 1968. Pantheon Books, NY.

*Marjorie Hansen Shaevitz. The Superwoman Syndrome. Copyright © 1984 by Marjorie Hansen
    Shaevitz. Warner Books Inc., NY.

*Maude. From the movie, "Harold and Maude." Copyright 1989, Paramount Corp., Hollywood, CA.

*Mother Jones. Ms. Magazine, November 1981, Copyright ©1981.

Mother Teresa. "Saints Among Us," Time Magazine, 29 Dec. 1975.

Muriel Rukeyser. The Life of Poetry. Copyright © 1949. Kraus, Millwood, NY.

Naomi Littlebear. Like A Mountain. Copyright © 1976.

*Ntozake Shange. "a laying on of hands," from For Colored Girls Who Have Considered Suicide/When
    The Rainbow is Enuf. Copyright © 1977, Ntozake Shange. Macmillian, NY.

Optimum Health Institute, Dr. Mark Solomon. 1993 Calendar.

Og Mandino. From The Choice. Copyright © 1984 by Og Mandino. Used by permission of Bantam
    Books, a division of Bantam Doubleday Dell Publishing Group, Inc.

Raisa Davydovna Orlova. Memoirs, Samuel Cioran, tr. Copyright © 1983. Random House, Inc., NY.

*Raya Dunayevskaya. "We Speak in Many Voices," Notes on Women's Liberation, Copyright © 1970.

*Richard Bach. Illusions. Copyright © 1981 by Richard Bach and Leslie Parrish-Bach.

*Robin Morgan. Ms. Magazine, July/August, 1993, Copyright © 1993.

*R.S. Read, J.D. Shouldn't You Be A Healer? A Manual for People Who Serve Life. Copyright © 1986.
    P.E.A.K.E., Huntington Beach, CA.

Ruth Beebe Hill. 'Hanta Yo': The Book of the Indian. Copyright © 1979, Ruth Beebe Hill,
    Doubleday, NY.

Shelagh Delaney. A Taste of Honey. Copyright © 1987. Grove-Atlic Press, NY.

*Simone de Beauvoir. <u>All Said and Done.</u> Copyright © 1974. Putnam Publishing Group, Inc., NY.
Also, as quoted in <u>The Women's Eye</u> by Anne Tucker. Copyright © 1973. Knopf, dist. by Random House.

Sophie Tucker. From an Anniversary Speech, 13 Jan. 1964. Wm. Morris Agency, NY.

*Sonia Johnson. <u>Going Out of Our Minds.</u> Copyright © 1987. The Crossing Press, Freedom, CA.

*Terry Cole-Whittaker. <u>What You Think Of Me Is None Of My Business.</u> Copyright © 1979, Terry Cole-Whittaker. Oak Tree Publications.

*Tina Turner. <u>What's Love Got to do With It?</u> Capitol Records, Inc., Hollywood, CA.

Victoria Billings. <u>The Womansbook,</u> "A Love to Believe In." Copyright © 1974. Wollstonecraft, Inc.

*<i>Wake Up and Dream,</i> <u>Spirit of Love...A Bouquet of Inspiring Songs.</u> Awakening Heart Productions. Copyright Skinny Music, Ed Tossing Music, Wireless Music.

Woititz, Janet G. <u>Struggle for Intimacy.</u> Copyright © 1985. Health Communications, Inc., Dearfield Beach, FL.